# Terry DeLapp

## *California Reveries*

September 9–October 2, 2004

# Spanierman Gallery, LLC

www.spanierman.com

45 East 58th Street    New York, NY 10022

Tel (212) 832-0208    Fax (212) 832-8114    gavin@spanierman.com

Terry DeLapp's creative evolution has followed rather a reverse path to that followed by many California artists of his generation. Instead of developing from a "traditional" to a more "conceptual," or spatially experimental style—in the manner of a painter such a Wayne Thiebaud—his work has tended toward the ever more classical. From a period in which DeLapp employed insistently (if subtly) political imagery, he has metamorphosed into a true California landscape painter.

But to characterize these recent landscapes and still lifes as truly representational is to wholly misrepresent them. Contrary to first impression, DeLapp is not a plein-air artist. His compositions are registered in nature, but executed in the studio. His space and light are essentially imaginary—and in this lies the key to their singularity. DeLapp's landscapes may be said to be metaphors for what is seen in the beautiful environment of coastal Central California. Their space and light are evoked reductively. They emerge from the sensibility of the artist, rather than from any "objective" reality. And yet we feel in them the precise quality of the place that has inspired them. The sky and foreground and architectural middleground of such paintings as *Barn and Yellow Field* (Cat. 7) or *Below the Mesa, Nipomo* (Cat. 1), are constructed in such a way as to bring the viewer directly into their separate worlds of light and atmosphere. We extrapolate time of day—high noon or dusk—from a fundamentally artificial, yet mysteriously persuasive, use of palette and perspective. If one has spent any time in or around Cambria, where the painter has lived and worked since 1992, one knows exactly what has so powerfully captured DeLapp's obsessively wrought images. Through them one even senses the region's slight, lambent odor of inland salt air.

The still lifes, of course, embody different qualities. In comparing them to the landscapes, it seems likely that they have followed from the landscapes or been somehow derived, spatially and chromatically, from those more complex works. Rather than summoning the structural and atmospheric character of the long landscape tradition stretching at least as far back as Constable or Claude Lorrain, the still lifes seem more fundamentally modern. It is not to Chardin, but to Morandi that they resonate. In a picture like *Pink Roses* (Cat. 4), representation takes second place to impression. The acrylic paint is put down with the most meticulous care and labor, resulting in the illusion of ease and quickness. DeLapp's mastery of facture and color in this medium which has proved intractable in most artists' hands, here becomes unexceptionable. The still lifes are somehow at once less seemingly imaginary than the landscapes, and more formally contrived in the service of sheer elegance. The use of a fairly exaggerated horizontal format, as in the masterly *Protea and Korean Dish* (Cat. 10), or the opulent *Purple Glads* (Cat. 6), creates an ingeniously decorative matrix in which to show off his elongated subject. The more conventionally scaled *Pink Roses* and *Dahlia and Mason Jar* (Cat. 2) are, oddly, no less distinctive in their exact rightness of scale and proportion.

I have rarely seen an artist make better use of the acrylic medium. As an admitted champion of oil paint, I come to DeLapp's work with a prejudice perhaps owing to my long study of the work of Richard Diebenkorn, for whom oil paint was always necessary. So it is with surprise that one comes to view DeLapp's chosen medium as not truly comparable to or preferable to oil paint, but instead, as perfectly suited to the particular range of color and texture he is inventing for his own vocabulary. DeLapp virtually makes this medium his own.

Terry DeLapp happens to live in one of the most bucolic and physically ravishing parts of the world. And yet it is also one of the most poignant environments in the world, given its transitory quality. Central California is yet unravaged. But the huge region which lies to its south, stretching virtually from San Diego to Santa Barbara, has been sickeningly transmogrified by development and highways. For someone who, like myself, grew up in the 1950s among the miles of citrus groves framed by the clearly visible, snow-capped San Gabriel Mountains, summering at the incomparable beach community of Laguna, the present-day character of those places is nothing short of heartbreaking. The constant pall of air pollution, cleansed only a few days a year by Santa Ana winds, settles over mile after mile of ugly housing developments. Even the

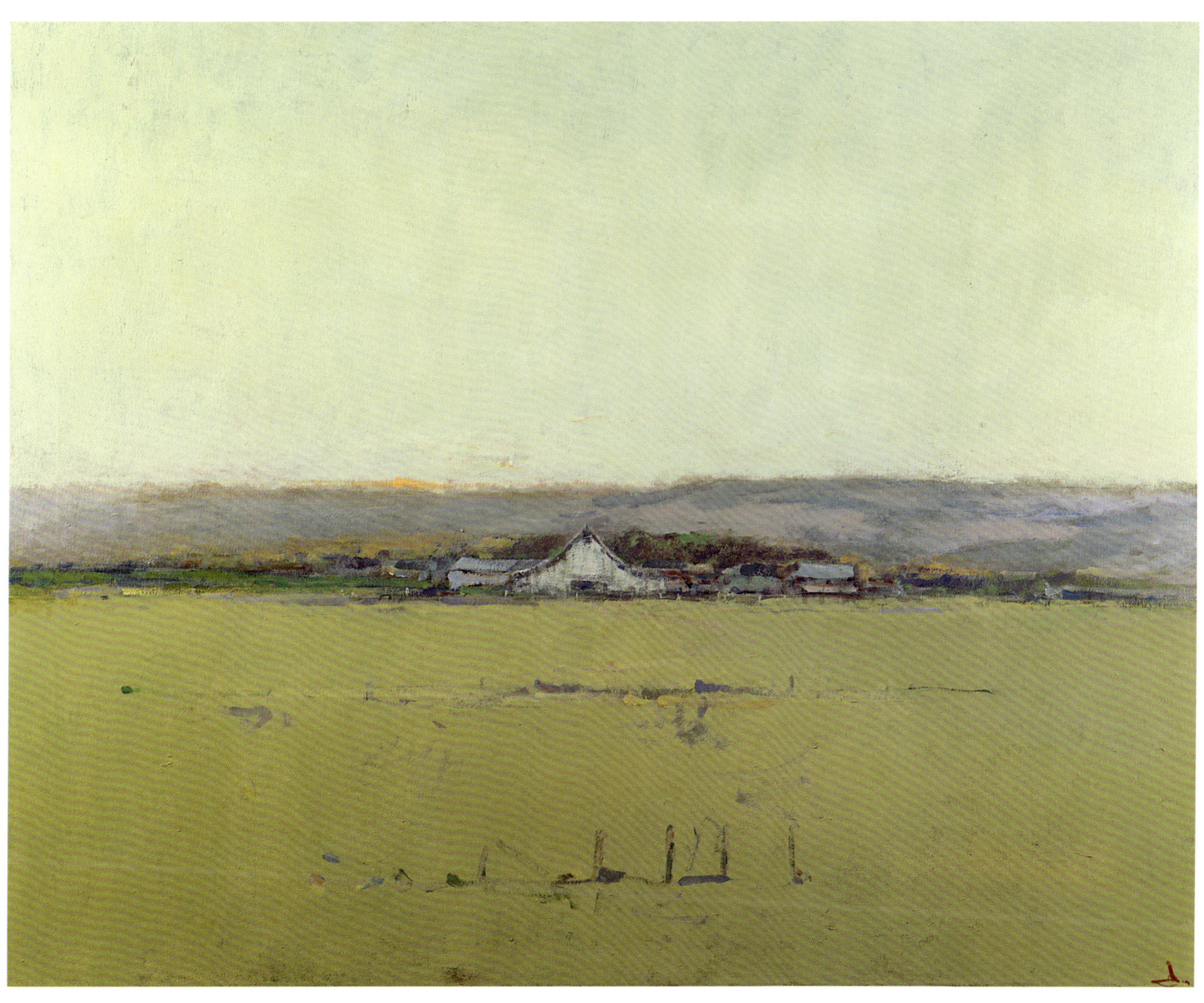

1. *Below the Mesa, Nipomo,* 2003

Acrylic on canvas, 40 × 50 inches. Signed with the artist's monogrammed initials lower right: *TDL*;
inscribed on verso: *Below the Mesa, Nipomo*

beach communities are choked with densely built housing, transient commercial neighborhoods, and smog. DeLapp's evocations of the tranquil beauty of the still unspoiled farmland to the north speak to me of both longing and sadness. Their appeal lies not so much in simple decorativeness or pull toward serene contemplation, as in their inescapable, underlying darkness. They show us scenes that cannot stay. They remind us that it is too late.

JANE LIVINGSTON

Jane Livingston is an independent author and curator whose work has ranged widely over many aspects of modern and contemporary art. As chief curator of the Corcoran Gallery of Art in Washington, D.C., from 1975 to 1989, she organized exhibitions and authored accompanying catalogues ranging from *Black Folk Art in America, 1930–1980* (1989) to *Hispanic Art in the United States: Thirty Contemporary Painters and Sculptors* (1987), as well as exhibitions on the work of photographers Manuel Alvarez Bravo (1979) and Lee Miller (1989). Recent major books include *The New York School: Photographs, 1936–1963* (1992), and the exhibition catalogue *Richard Avedon: Evidence 1944–1994* (1994). Livingston's exhibition catalogues also include *The Art of Richard Diebenkorn* (1997) and *The Paintings of Joan Mitchell* (2002), both for the Whitney Museum of American Art.

---

*Born in Pasadena in 1934, Terry DeLapp studied at the Chouinards Art Academy in Hollywood and at the University of California. DeLapp currently lives and works in Cambria, California. He has been exhibiting his paintings since the early 1980s, participating in group shows in California, New Mexico and elsewhere. DeLapp has had numerous solo exhibitions as well, most recently at the Bakersfield Museum of Art (1998). His paintings can be found at the San Diego Museum of Art, and in many private collections, including those of Steve Martin, Martin Mull, Joan Rivers, Julian Ganz, and Robert Zemeckis.*

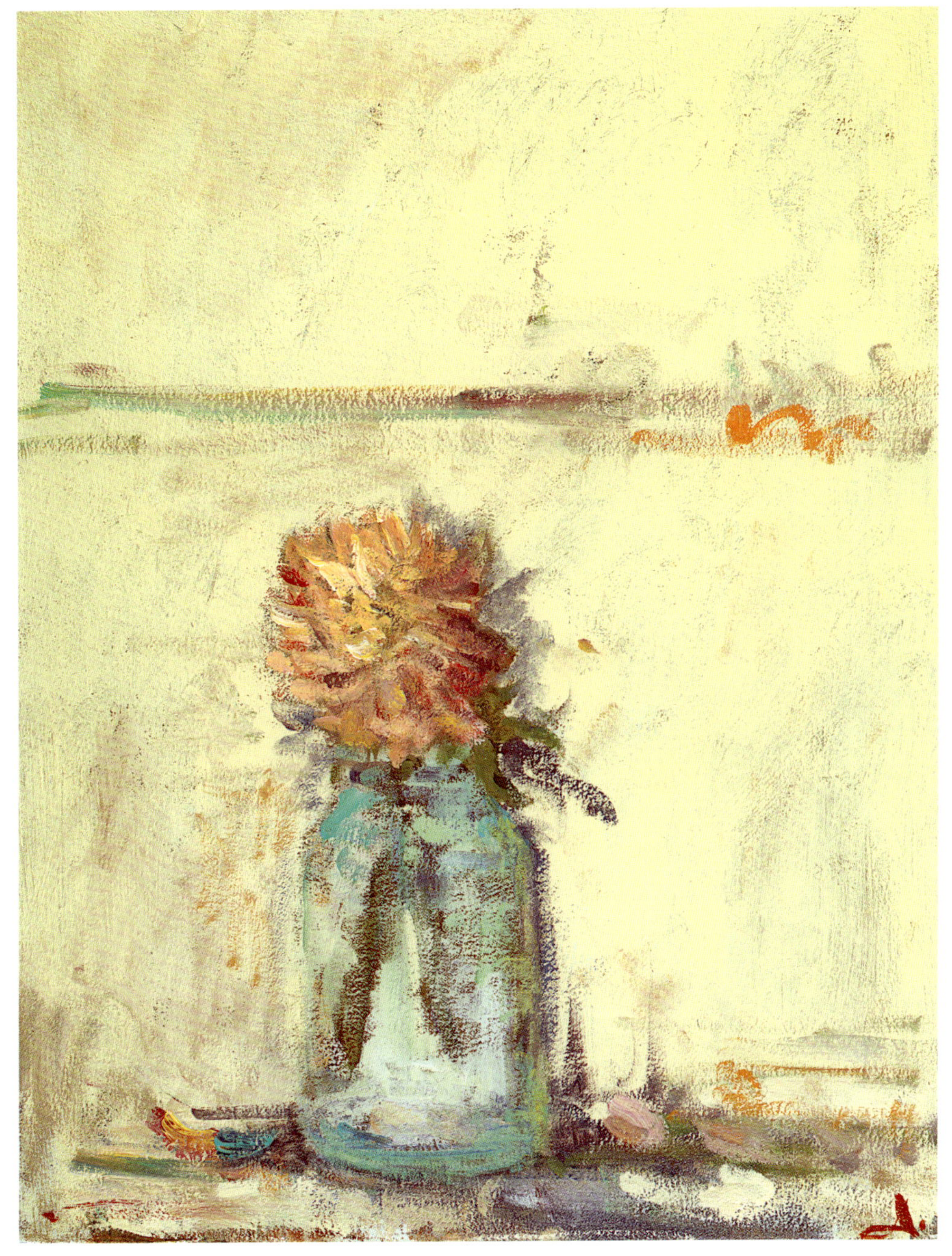


2. *Dahlia and Mason Jar,* 2003
Acrylic on canvas, 20 × 16 inches. Signed with the artist's monogrammed initials lower right: *TDL;*
inscribed on verso: *Dahlia and Mason Jar*

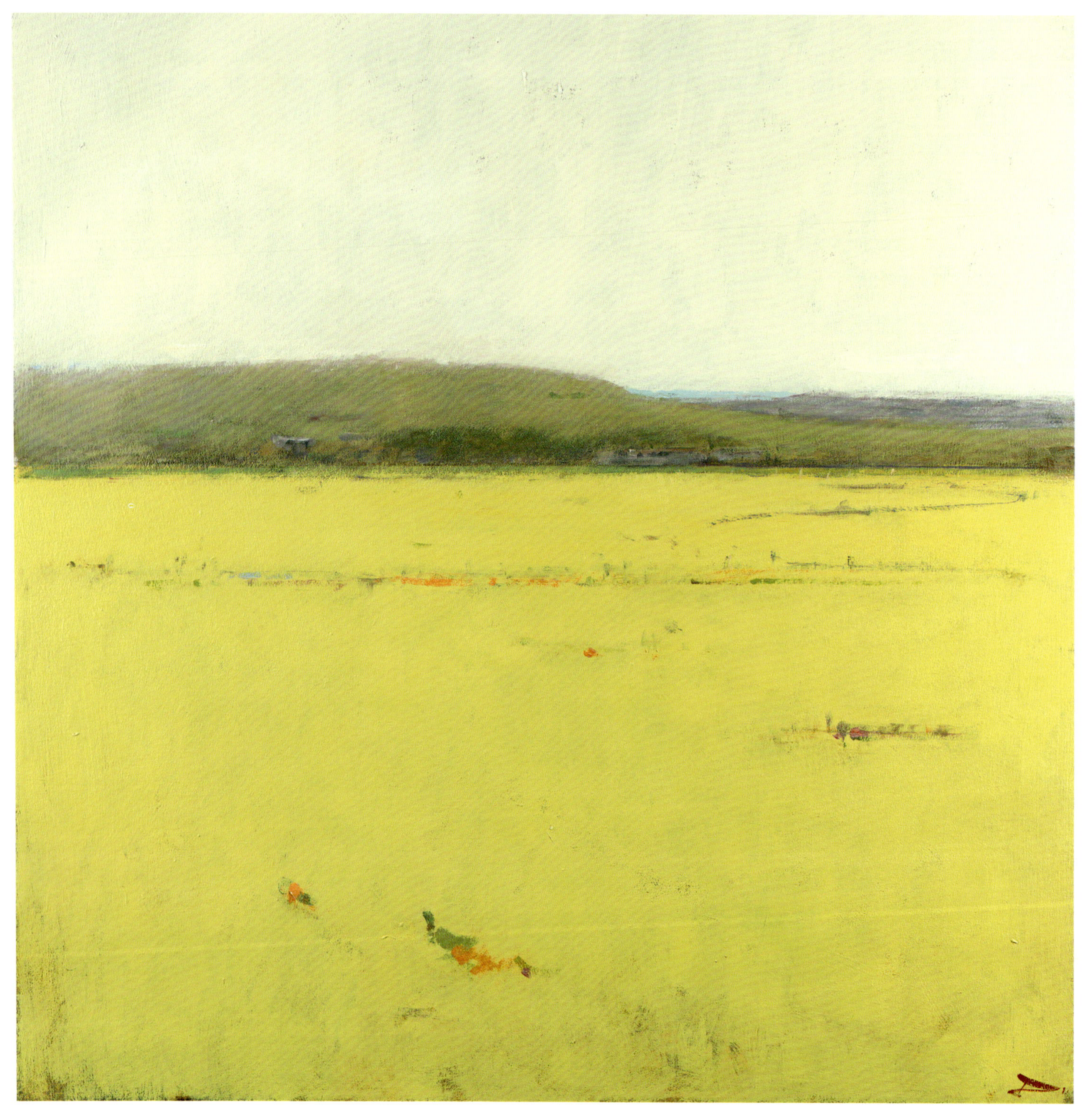

3. *Mustard Field—Taylor Ranch,* 2004

Acrylic on canvas, 36 × 36 inches. Signed with the artist's monogrammed initials lower right: *TDL*;
inscribed on verso: *Mustard Field—Taylor Ranch*

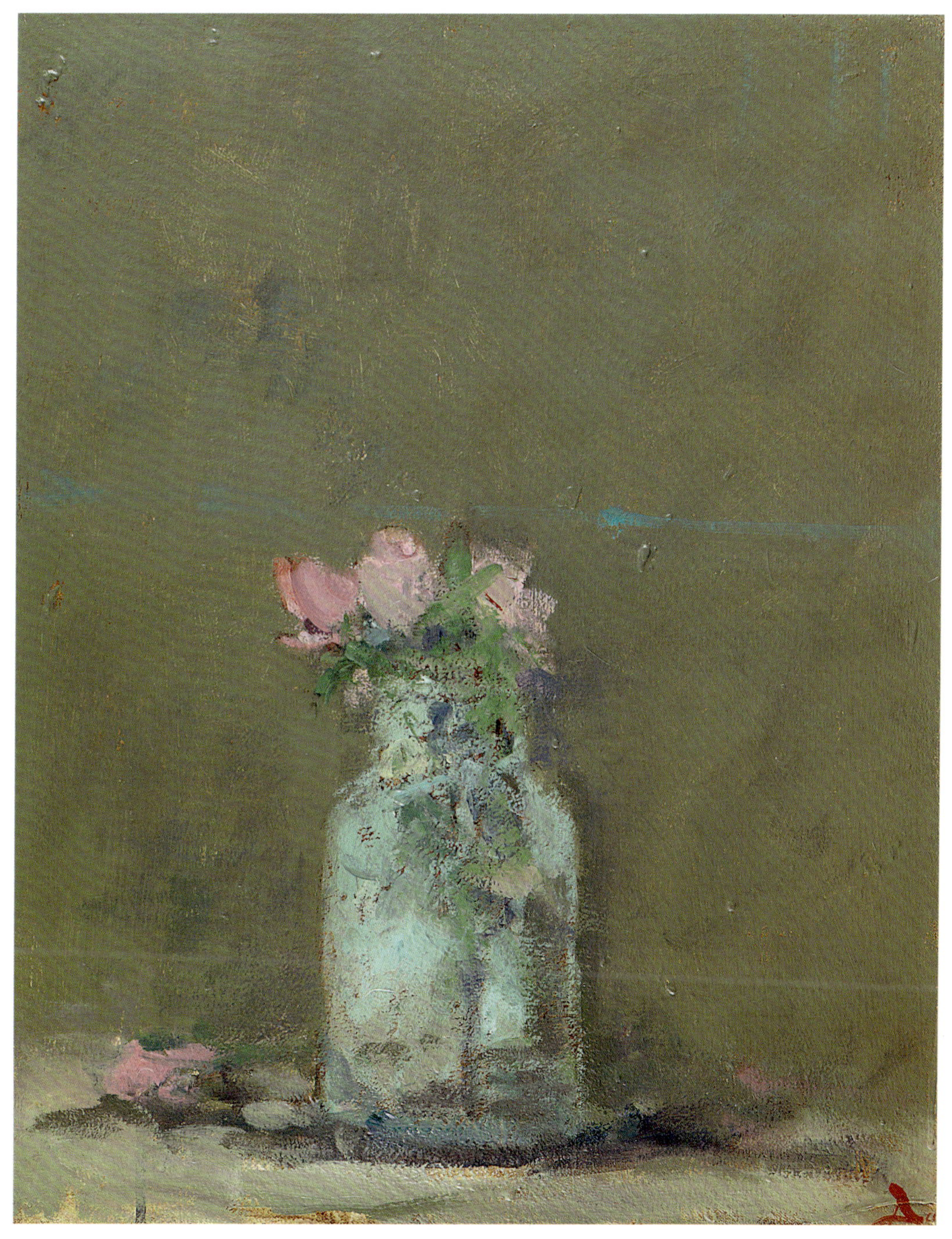

4. *Pink Roses,* 2003

Acrylic on canvas, 20 × 16 inches. Signed with the artist's monogrammed initials lower right: *TDL*;
inscribed on verso: *Pink Roses*

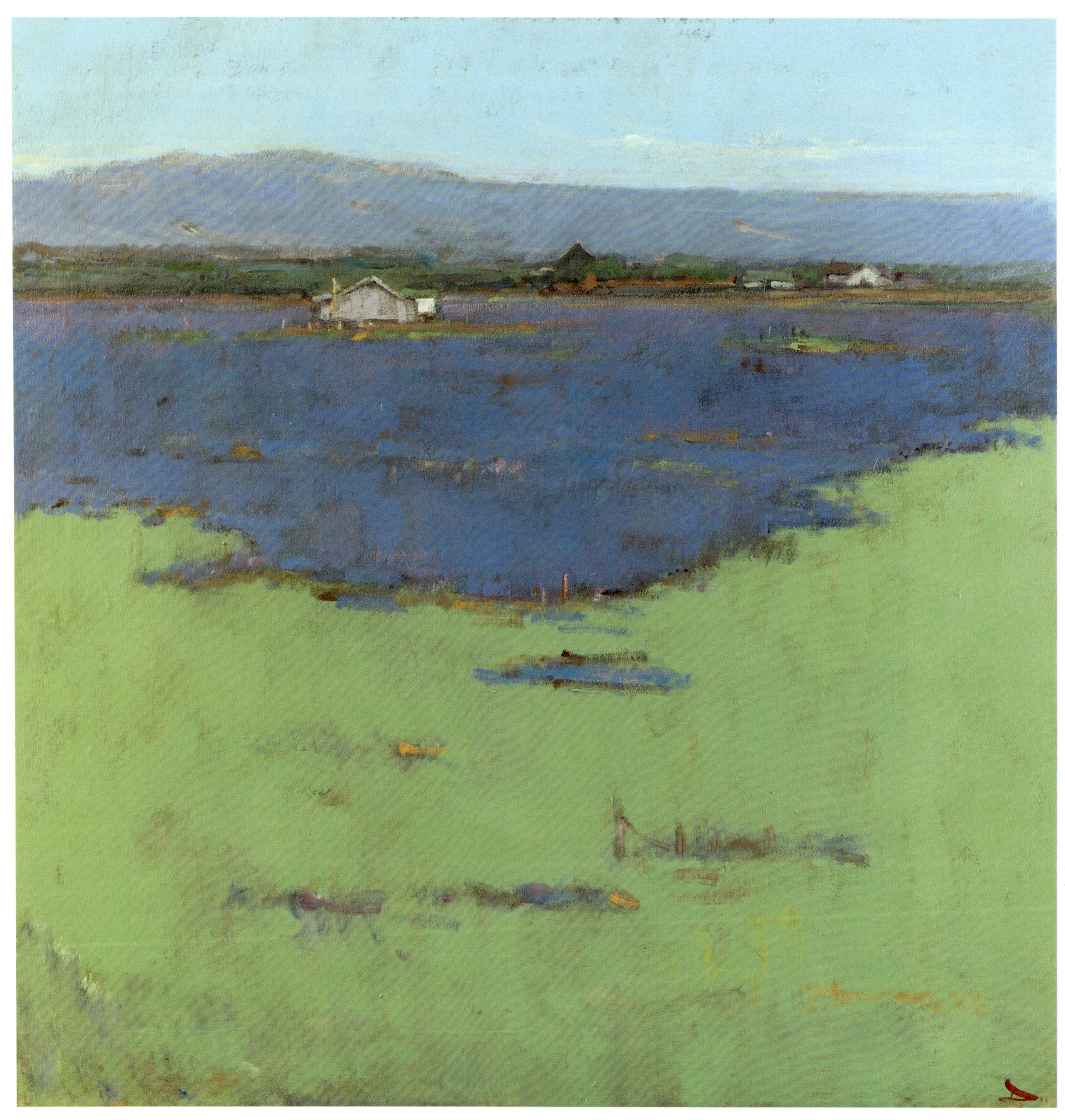

5. *Wild Lupine and White Barn*, 2004

Acrylic on canvas, 36 × 36 inches. Signed with the artist's monogrammed initials lower right: *TDL*;
inscribed on verso: *Wild Lupine and White Barn*

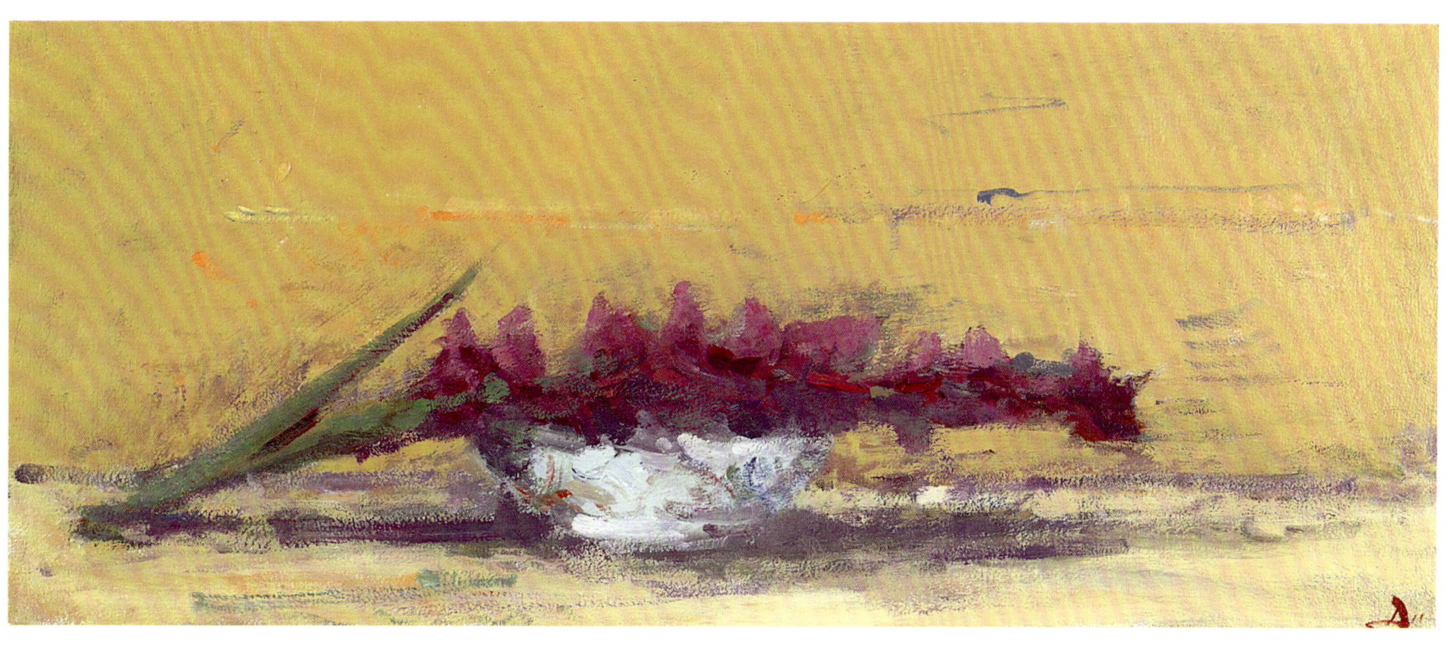

6.  *Purple Glads,* 2002

Acrylic on canvas, 12 × 28 inches. Signed with the artist's monogrammed initials lower right: *TDL*;
inscribed on verso: *Purple Glads*

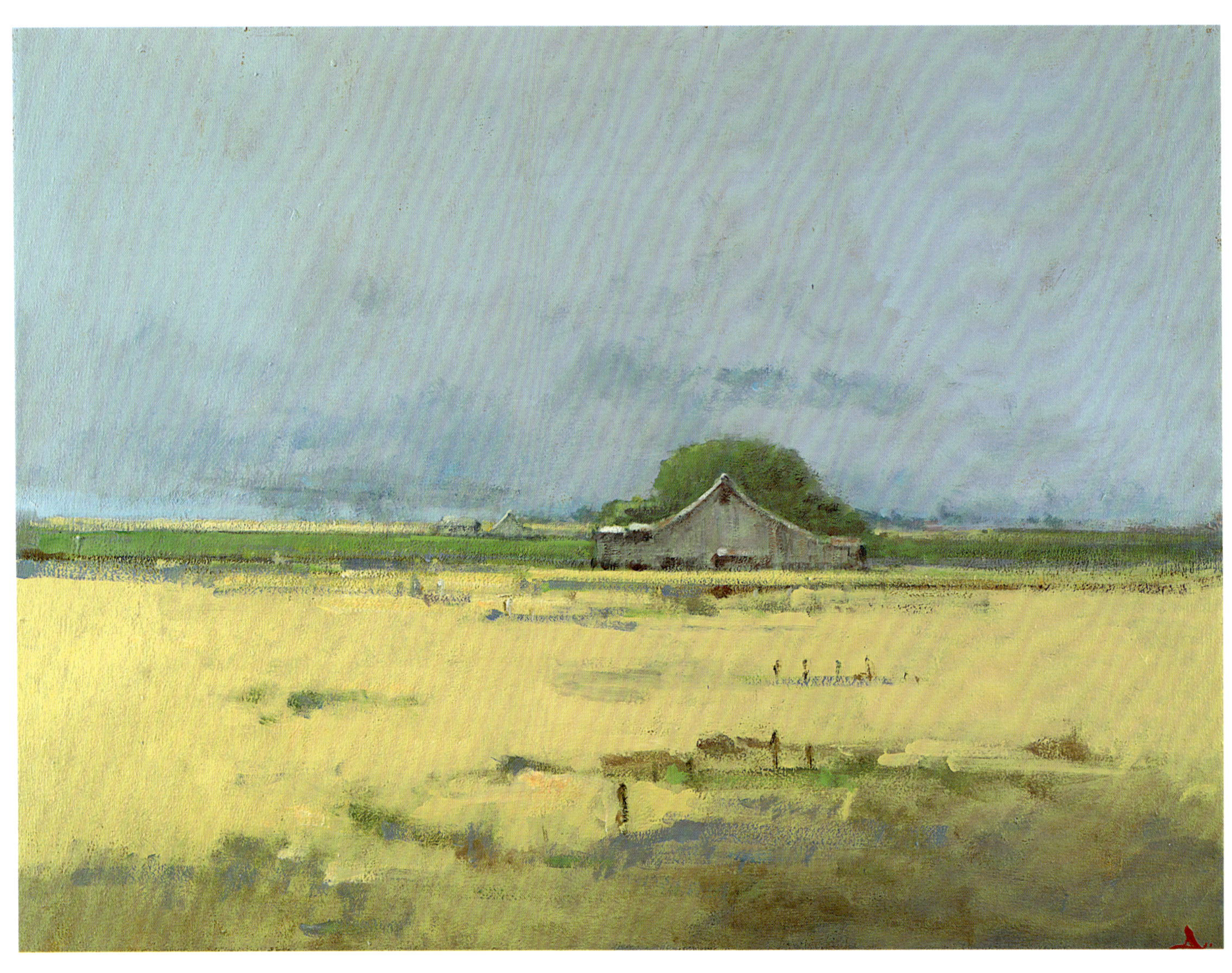

7.  *Barn and Yellow Field,* 2003

Acrylic on canvas, 24 × 32 inches. Signed with the artist's monogrammed initials lower right: *TDL*;
inscribed on verso: *Barn and Yellow Field*

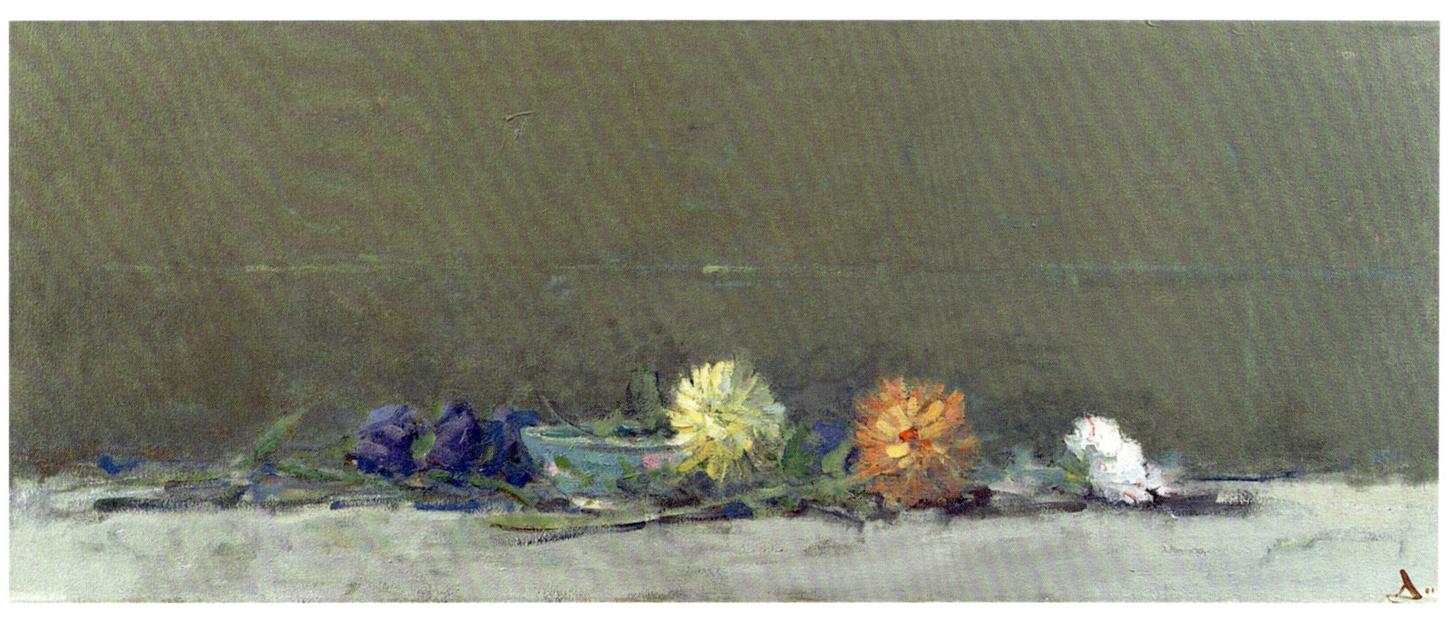

8. *Dahlia, Iris, Carnation, and Nightshade,* 2002

Acrylic on canvas, 16 × 40 inches. Signed with the artist's monogrammed initials lower right: *TDL*;
inscribed on verso: *Dahlia, Iris, Carnation and Nightshade*

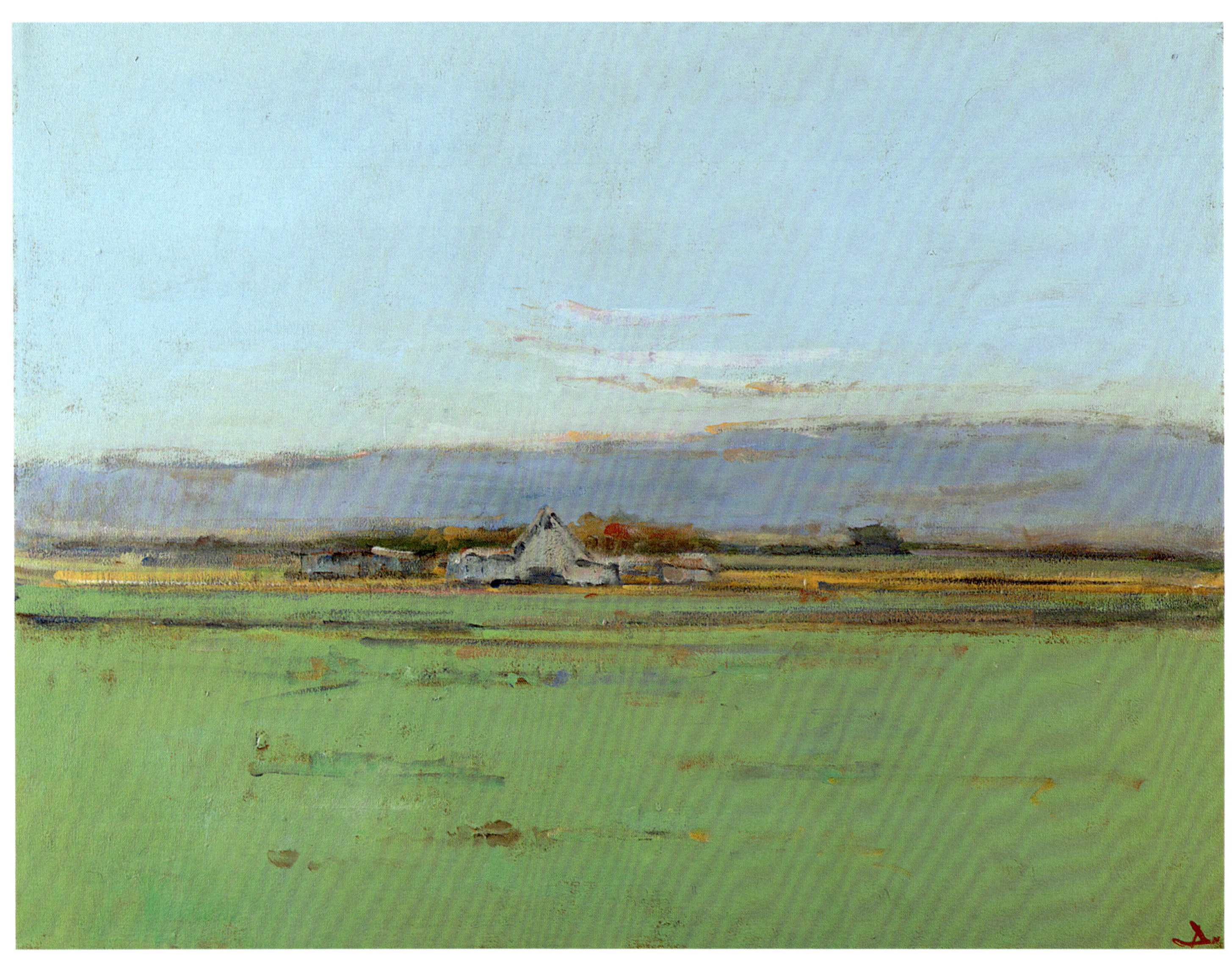

9. *Big Farm—I,* 2002

Acrylic on canvas, 24 × 32 inches. Signed with the artist's monogrammed initials lower right: *TDL*; inscribed on verso: *Big Farm—I*

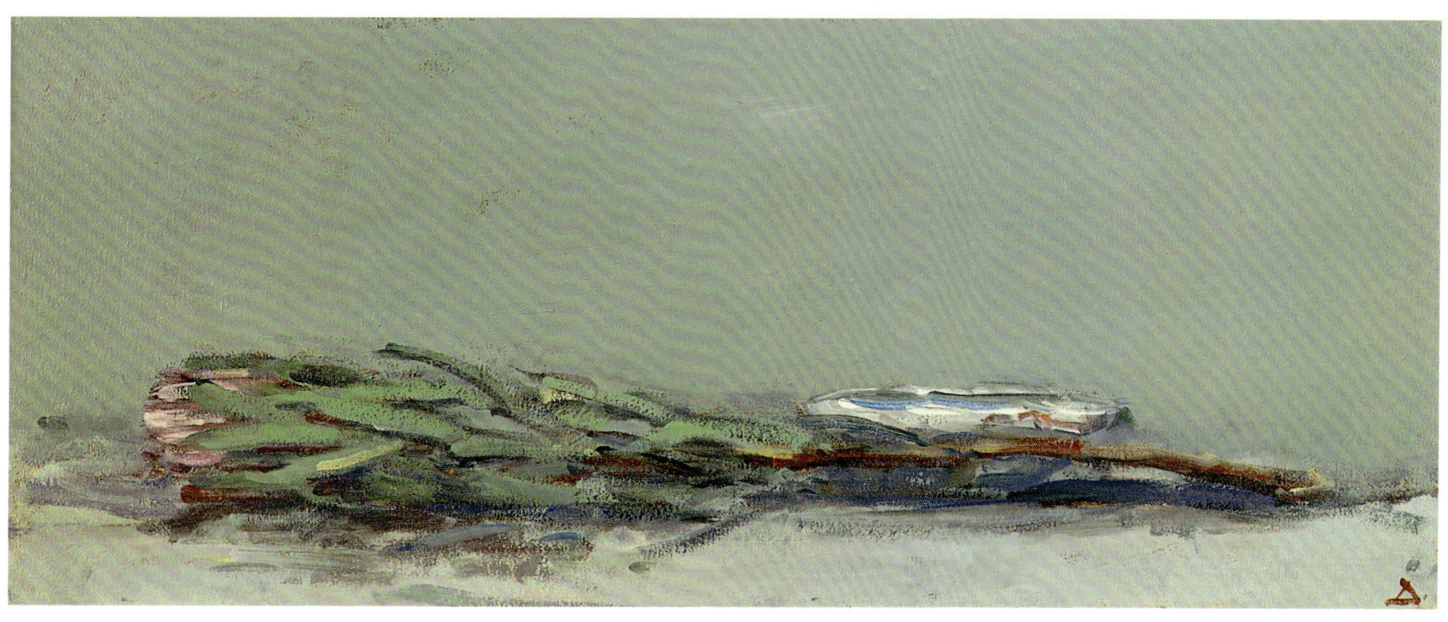

10.  *Protea and Korean Dish,* 2001

Acrylic on canvas, 11 × 27 inches. Signed with the artist's monogrammed initials lower right: *TDL*

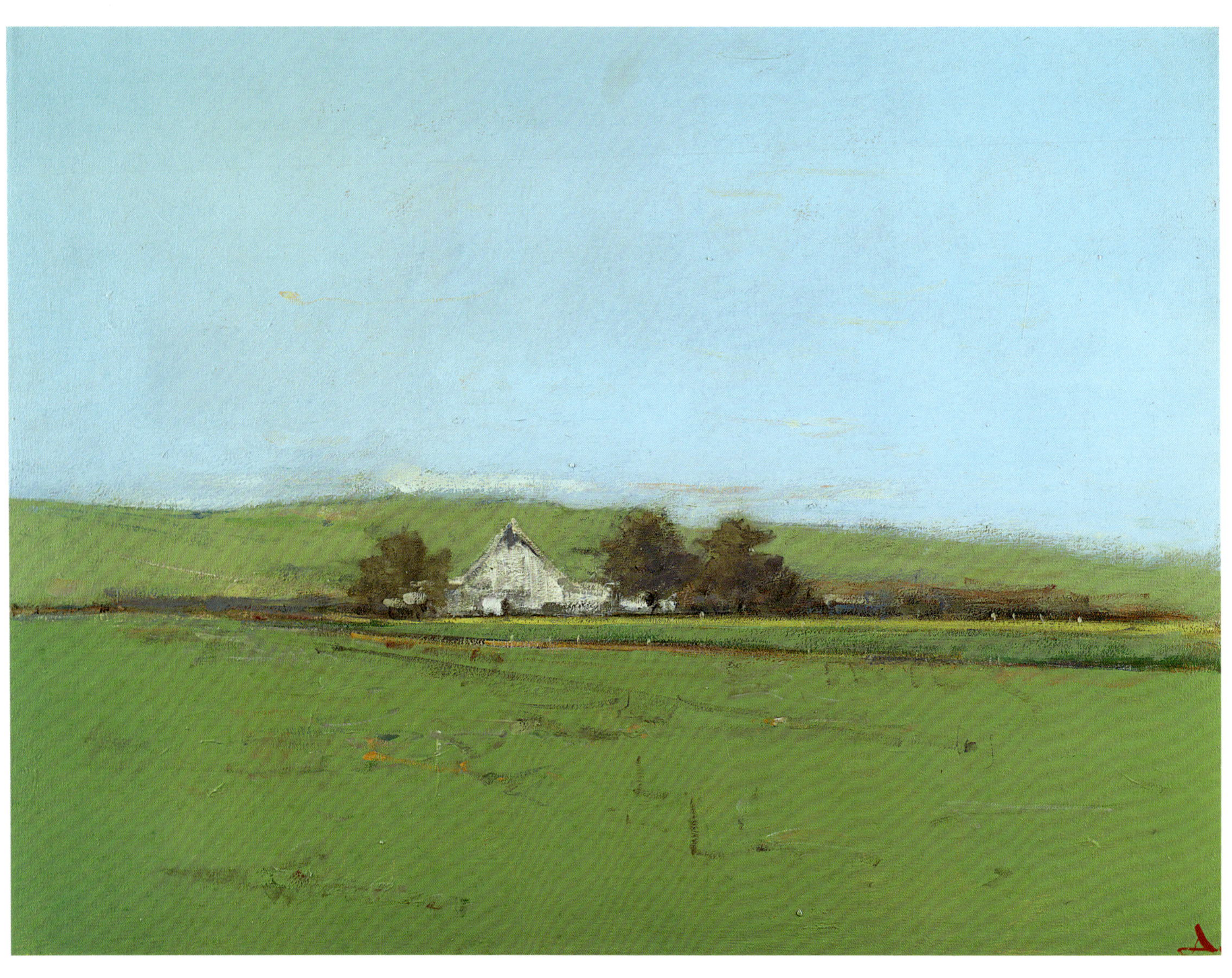

11.  *White Barn, Old Creek Road,* 2003

Acrylic on canvas, 24 × 32 inches. Signed with the artist's monogrammed initials lower right: *TDL*;
inscribed on verso: *White Barn, Old Creek Road*

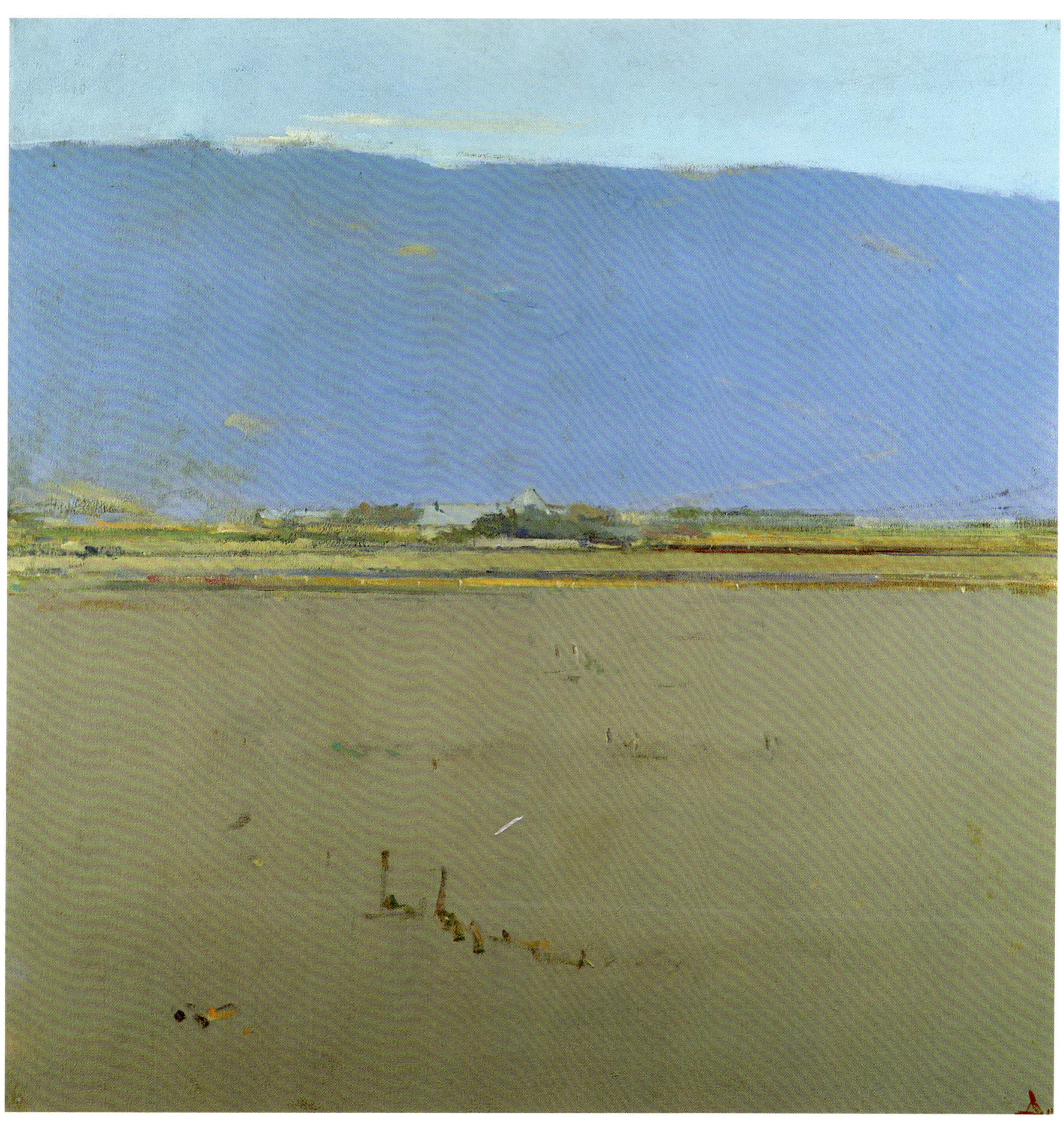

12.  *Bear Mountain, Afternoon,* 2003

Acrylic on canvas, 36¼ × 36¼ inches. Signed with the artist's monogrammed initials lower right: *TDL*;<br>inscribed on verso: *Bear Mountain Afternoon*

# Index to Illustrations